Jenny Mosley's

# Circle Time Handbook

## for the Golden Rules stories

Helping children with social and
emotional aspects of learning

Illustrations by Juliet Doyle
from the Golden Rules storybooks
by Donna Luck and Juliet Doyle

**Positive Press**

*With thanks to Juliet Doyle and Donna Luck for their invaluable contribution to this book*

Published 2005 by:

Positive Press Ltd
28A Gloucester Road
Trowbridge
BA14 0AA
Telephone: 01225 719204
Fax: 01225 712187
Email: positivepress@jennymosley.co.uk
Web site: www.circle-time.co.uk

Text © Jenny Mosley
Illustrations © Juliet Doyle

ISBN 190-4866-123

Printed by:
Heron Press
19-24 White Hays North
West Wilts Trading Estate
Westbury
Wiltshire
BA13 4JT

# Contents

# THE GOLDEN RULES

We listen to people, we don't interrupt

We are honest, we don't cover up the truth

We are kind and helpful, we don't hurt anybody's feelings

We are gentle, we don't hurt others

We try to work hard, we don't waste time

We look after property, we don't waste or damage things

# How to use this book

Miss Beanie

This handbook is designed to be used alongside the six storybooks about Miss Beanie and her class of lovable characters. The message in each story is reinforced with two full circle meetings and four extension activities for each Golden Rule. The following tips will help you to get the most from the activities and games in each chapter.

- **Read each story before you begin planning** so that you are familiar with the characters and the plot.

- **Select and adapt your approach to circle time.** Read 'How Circle Time Works' on page 6-7 so that you are clear about the reasons behind the five stages but remember that not all of your children are going to be ready to participate in full circle meetings. Provided you do a warm-up at the beginning and end each meeting on a positive note, you can pick and mix the steps depending on what you think your children need and can cope with.

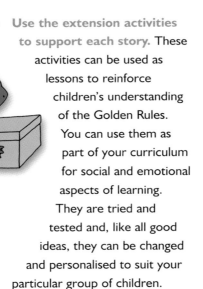

- **Use the extension activities to support each story.** These activities can be used as lessons to reinforce children's understanding of the Golden Rules. You can use them as part of your curriculum for social and emotional aspects of learning. They are tried and tested and, like all good ideas, they can be changed and personalised to suit your particular group of children.

Alfred Alligator

- **Let the children explore each rule.** It is important that the children have plenty of opportunities to play and invent their own scenarios around the Golden Rules. Structured play with puppets can help them to express individual feelings and ideas. It will give you the opportunity to discuss how we all see and feel things differently and how we show respect for our differences.

- **Use puppets to bring the characters to life.** If you have fluffy animal toys or big animal puppets you can use them to bring the stories alive. They can be co-opted to explain the activities that reinforce the moral concepts behind each Golden Rule. If you haven't used puppets before, you will find that they can be a magical experience and are easy to use once you have practised.

  - In front of a mirror, try out the different moods that you want your puppet to express.

  - Remember that your puppet needs to make eye contact with your audience in the same way that a real person would.

  - Allow your puppet to be still just like a real person – it doesn't need to be constantly moving.

- **Use finger puppets to support the stories.** Young children find finger puppets easy to operate and they quickly learn to speak for the puppets. This increases their involvement in the stories and ensures that each Golden Rule is reviewed and reinforced in a natural but effective manner. A set of finger puppet characters is available to buy to complement this book, but you can make a set of finger puppet characters cheaply and simply using old gloves. Just cut off the fingers and attach faces made from felt to them to make different characters. (You can either sew on the features or use a fabric pen.) Alternatively, make little tubes from paper which can be decorated by hand. Use crayons, or any suitable materials such as fur fabric, to help create the characters. Here are some tips to help the children make the best use of their finger puppets:

  - Give your class time to explore the puppets by keeping them on an activity table and offering the opportunity for play and invention of stories for each puppet.

Louis Lion

# How to use this book

Mona Monkey

- Ensure that the children match the puppets to the story characters with prompts such as, 'Look at the little elephant. She's called Elsa. I think she looks friendly. What do you think?'

- Invite a child to hold, move and speak for one of the puppets and encourage the rest of the group to ask questions such as, 'Mona, do you like cornflakes?' or 'What is your favourite dinner?' You can develop this by talking more about feelings, 'Mona, how do you feel when you hear thunder?'

- **Make the puppets part of your class.** You can sustain your children's interest by using the characters as part of a short daily ritual. For example, Mona could be very mischievous and each morning you could play 'I-spy' and see if the children can spot what Mona has done in the room over night – hidden the pencils, turned a poster upside down, left a half-eaten biscuit on a table and so on.

- **Develop the characters.** When the children play with the storybook characters, a stream of new information will be generated. This can be added to a storyboard and used to extend their vocabulary. Write the name of the character in the centre of a poster-sized sheet of paper and display each piece of information around the name. Each group will assemble a unique set of facts, and it might include things like this: likes to play with dolls, likes to eat jam, dances when she is happy, and so on.

# How circle time works

The aim of Quality Circle Time is to nurture children's social and emotional growth and strengthen their self-esteem. Although each meeting is planned and directed by the adult circle time leader, its aim is to encourage children to interact with confidence because each individual is given the opportunity to contribute to the group and feels supported by other members. This helps everyone to work as a team which celebrates difference in others and respects their values and beliefs. Regular circle meetings help children to become emotionally strengthened, socially confident and able to cope with the stresses and strains of life.

These outcomes can only happen if an atmosphere of trust is established from the very beginning of each meeting. For this reason, each session begins with two introductory phases that are designed to help the children into the correct frame of mind. Key issues can then be investigated until the time comes to wind down the meeting. Two further phases lighten the mood and ensure that everyone feels safe, comfortable and ready for the next part of the school day.

Each circle time session begins with everyone seated to form a circle and facing the centre.

### STEP 1 Meeting up – playing a game

Begin each meeting with a fun warm-up activity or opening game. This helps the children to relax and feel the pleasure of being together. It often involves a game that requires the children to change places so that they find themselves sitting with classmates who are not their usual companions. This gives them the opportunity to make new friends and helps to build group identity.

These games need to be played quickly and need not take more than a few minutes. For some classes, it is best not to start with a highly energetic game: a more relaxing activity like 'Pass a thumbs-up' may be chosen.

### STEP 2 Warming up – breaking the silence

This step is designed to remind children that they all have the right to speak and the responsibility of listening during circle time. The circle leader makes this as straightforward as possible by giving the group the beginning of a sentence, for example, 'My favourite colour is…' Each child repeats this beginning and completes it with a word of their choice. This is called a 'round'.

A 'speaking object' is used to show whose turn it is to speak. Whoever is holding it has the right to speak uninterrupted. The speaking object is then passed to the next person. This object needs to be small enough to fit into little hands: a painted wooden egg is often used. A small, fluffy toy works well, or an object can be chosen to fit in with topic work.

Holding the speaking object does not oblige anyone to speak and any child who does not wish to do so may say 'pass' and hand it on. However, some children often say 'pass' because they don't have the confidence or they are testing out the teacher. It is possible, the day before circle time, to tell children what the round is going to be and give them a chance to prepare what they want to say on a small card. If a child finds it difficult to get a sentence ready you may need to give them a little help before the meeting begins. Very young children can be shy and it is often a good idea to sit in a small circle, before the big circle time, with a puppet who chats to children about what will happen in circle time and offers to speak for the child if he is shy.

### STEP 3 — Opening up - exploring issues that concern the class

Now that the children are relaxed and have practised speaking and listening, they are ready to tackle the most challenging phase of the meeting. This is sometimes called 'open forum' because it is an opportunity to express opinions and discuss important issues.

This middle phase is vital for encouraging children to develop a belief in their ability to make responsible choices and decisions. Problem-solving skills can be rehearsed and targets can be agreed. It is important that children remember to raise their hands (or make a 'thumbs-up') before speaking, speak one at a time and listen to each other. Many practitioners teach children to use the following prompts:

**Child:** 'I need help because…'
**Teacher/peers:** 'Would it help if I…?' or 'Would it help if you…?'

Alternatively, this phase may be used to investigate and practise specific skills. Some children are not ready to take responsibility for their actions or to have a spotlight of attention shone on them.

Zelda Zebra

Elsa Elephant

It is advisable for some teachers to explore the use of metaphor to help children discuss difficult issues. Stories, role-play, games, puppets, the dressing-up box and other props can be used to help children to sensitively explore problems, concerns, hopes or fears.

### STEP 4 — Cheering up - celebrating the positive

Before a circle time session finishes, it is important to move the children away from the issues of concern that were investigated in the middle phase of the meeting. The 'cheering up' phase is used to celebrate the group's successes and strengths and give praise and thanks to one another. This can be immediate praise for the work the children have done in the meeting or can include a more general celebration of recent school accomplishments.

You could also use this step to allow children to cheer up by learning something new. Children can go into the middle of the circle and teach everyone a new playground game. In short, this step makes people feel more competent, happy and positive.

### STEP 5 — Calming down - bridging children forward

It is crucial that children experience quiet and calm before they leave the classroom to go to another activity. This activity is called 'bridging': you are helping a child to experience a closing ritual so that the transition to the next part of their day is smooth and successful. Some teachers play a very calm game like 'pass the tambourine without a sound'. Alternatively, a guided visualisation, 'mood' music, or a rain-stick can be used to introduce simple meditation techniques to your group. In this way, you touch the children's imagination thereby strengthening their inner core. What they learn through this step is that they have sufficient inner resources to calm down and make themselves feel happy.

Allow around 45 minutes for a session involving all of the five steps. You can select activities from the five steps for a shorter version, but **NEVER** end on 'Opening up' (stage 3). It is essential that you provide a bridge from your work and discussion in this part of your circle time to the rest of the school day.

# What are the golden rules?

The moral values that we learn as children are part of the wider process of socialisation. Our sense of morality is grounded in our growing understanding that we must build bonds with other people to ensure our mutual well-being in a community. A consensus about the values that should underpin and guide our behaviour towards each other is the code of conduct that ensures that we can live in social harmony by taking care of one another.

Morality is linked to consequences. We decide if an action is right or wrong when we see how it affects the people around us. Does it harm or improve their welfare?

By teaching moral standards that are universal, schools and parents are promoting behaviours that are common to all humanity. They should incorporate the moral codes of all the major religions without undercutting the particular practices that make them all different. The Quality Circle Time model considers these universal values to be vitally important and calls them the Golden Rules:

> We are gentle, we don't hurt others.
>
> We are kind and helpful,
> we don't hurt anybody's feelings.
>
> We are honest, we don't cover up the truth.
>
> We work hard, we don't waste time.
>
> We listen, we don't interrupt.
>
> We look after property, we don't damage things.

People often ask why there are negative statements in the Golden Rules. Young children learn through opposites. Hot and cold, smooth and rough: each concept's opposite enhances its 'definition' or knowledge of itself. We can put our emphasis on the positive part of the Golden Rule by scribing it in gold lettering and keeping the negative part in small, grey writing. But the negative is still there as a reverse image.

Everything depends on the language you use. An ideal approach might be as follows: 'Do you know the rule you are breaking now? By hurting Wayne, you are breaking the Golden Rule of being gentle'. The fact that all the adults share a mutual understanding of the rules is reinforced when the whole learning community, including the parents, use similar applications of the Golden Rules.

## Introducing the Golden Rules

For very young children it is advisable to start with two positive statements:

> We are gentle.
>
> We are kind.

There is a further Golden Rule that is useful for young children:

> We play well, we don't spoil each others' games.

The other Golden Rules can be introduced gradually from the second term of the reception year onwards.

Young children need visual images to support their learning. It is important that displays of the Golden Rules are surrounded by photographs of children showing gentle and kind behaviours. Firstly, you need to engage the children in discussions of what a gentle act and a kind act would look like. Eventually they will be able to describe examples of behaviour that they would like to see shown in photographs. Later, you can draw attention to the Golden Rules by pointing to the photographs.

## The benefits of using stories

We cannot be truly moral unless we are able to see things from another person's point of view. It is important that we help children to take the big cognitive leap from self-absorption to a sense of empathy and sharing that is called 'perspective taking'. Many children find this difficult, but practice makes perfect. This essential cognitive shift is accelerated by social interaction and games that draw attention to the skills involved. Another useful strategy is to harness children's imagination by using plays, stories and puppets to stimulate discussion about what is right and what is wrong.

In stories, the predicaments we all face are made concrete and the structure – a beginning, middle and end – means that children can experience the thrill of anticipation safe in the knowledge that all will be sorted out in the end.

Stories usually deal with action and its consequences and so provide excellent starting points for discussions about moral behaviour. The main characters are involved in goal-oriented action and we learn about the strategies they use to overcome hurdles and setbacks before they reach the satisfying place where stories end.

Interesting moral questions can be teased out from almost any children's story. However, the Golden Rules series makes each Golden Rule the subject of a separate story that has been written specifically with the needs of young children in mind. All you need to do is to read them to your group. A range of open-ended questions can then be asked to encourage them to build on the ideas embedded in the story. For example...

*'Can you tell me which of the Golden Rules was broken?'*

*'Why did he/she break the rule?'*

*'What happened because he/she broke the rule?'*

*'Why do you think the other characters reacted as they did?'*

*'How do you think the other characters felt when he/she did that?'*

*'What do you think should have happened to the character after he/she did that?'*

*'If you were the character, how do you think you would be feeling at that moment?'*

*'If you could change the story, how would it end?'*

*'Was it fair? Was it right?'*

These questions gently introduce children to philosophical dialogue and debate.

## Using finger puppets

Moral values can be difficult to talk about and there are many advantages to using finger puppets to open up discussion (see pages 4-5). When children are able to speak through a puppet they often find that they can say things that would be impossible to articulate if they were required to use their 'real' voice. In the same way, you will find that puppets are able to close the distance between you, as an adult, and the children with whom you wish to communicate. Once you have a finger puppet you can cross the generation gap and speak 'as a child'.

What is more, you can sit with a finger puppet and a script on your lap and nobody will complain – your audience will be so riveted by the puppet's antics that they won't even notice that you are reading!

## Learning to love the Golden Rules

The commitment of staff and children is of paramount importance if the Golden Rules are to be applied with confidence. This commitment requires that they are learned in an atmosphere of respect and that all parties understand why they are so important. To impose the Golden Rules is to show that you expect obedience but to negotiate them is to show that you desire co-operation and that you are ready to discuss all the uncertainties that your children may feel. By discussing the problems that your children encounter, you are also showing that you value their participation in creating an environment that is emotionally safe. This raises the communal sense of responsibility and increases the likelihood that your children will use these rules as life-long codes of conduct. You will be giving them something of inestimable value in helping them to become compassionate adults.

# We are gentle...

## Circle time session 1

use the five steps of circle time to explore the importance of being gentle to others

### Circle Time Session 1 Preparation

Look at the characters on the front cover. Do the children know their names? Have they seen them in other stories? Read the story until the end of page 15, then stop and ask the children if they can think of any ways in which Alfred could be helped when he returns to school. Read on to the end of the story.

### What you need

- A copy of the book We Are Gentle, We Don't Hurt Others
- Alfred Alligator and other animal finger puppets
- A speaking object

### Meeting up

- Go round the group and point to each child in turn and tell them that they are either Louis Lion, Gino Giraffe or Alfred Alligator. Now call out each name in turn. As each name is called, the children with that name must swap seats.

- You can do this more than once or you can call out, 'All the animals' and everybody must find a new place to sit.

### Warming up

- Put Alfred Alligator on your finger. Hide your hand in a pocket and use this script to introduce him to the children:

**Adult:** *Something is wriggling in my pocket. What could it be?*
(Take Alfred out of your pocket and hold him up for everyone to see.)

**Alfred:** *That's better; it was very stuffy in that pocket and now I can do a bit of climbing.*
(Help Alfred to climb up your arm.)

**Adult:** *Hey, where do you think you're going? If you look the other way, you will see some lovely children.*
(Turn to the children.)
*Look at his long green nose and his spiky green tail. Who can guess who this green animal is?*
(Take answers from the group.)
*Yes, this is Alfred Alligator. Say hello to the children, Alfred.*

**Alfred:** *Hello children! Who would like to come up here and stroke my scaly green tail?*

- Ask the children what they know about alligators and make a list of the facts they offer. Ask if any of them would like to be an alligator with scaly skin and very sharp teeth. What other animals might they prefer to be? Using the speaking object, ask the children to complete the sentence, 'If I were an animal, I would be…'

### Opening up

- Think of some situations that arise in your classroom and ask the children for ideas about how these could have been dealt with more gently. Situations could be similar to the following:

# We don't hurt others

*Gary couldn't get past Rebecca's chair so he pushed past and she fell off.*

*Freddie needed a rubber so Robbie threw it across the table and it hit Cara in the eye.*

*Carl wouldn't give Grace a pencil so she hit him.*

*Brad needed to get to the front of the carpet so he walked straight through everyone who was sitting down and trod on three people's fingers.*

*Jenny was trying to catch Claire in the playground but she grabbed her hood and Claire fell and hurt her knee.*

Let the children role-play these situations and show how each situation could have been resolved with gentleness. Encourage them to think of ideas and talk about how they could try to be gentler with each other.

## Cheering up

- Thank the children for their helpful suggestions. Be specific and thank individual children but give general thanks as well. Refer to acts of consideration and gentleness that you have recently observed in your classroom.

## Calming down

- Hold up your hands and let your fingers wiggle as you bring them down. At the same time, make a *shhh* sound. Tell the children that this is a gentle sound. Let them join in as you do it again. Turn to the child next to you, smile and make the sound again. Ask them to turn to the child next to them, smile and send the wiggle and gentle sound round the group.

# Circle time session 2

## Meeting up

- Put Alfred Alligator on your finger but keep him hidden.

- Ask the children if any of them know how to ride a bicycle. Talk about what fun bikes can be, but allow Alfred to distract you by tapping your cheek. Turn to look at him and hold a conversation that could begin like this:

## The story

*Miss Beanie is shocked to find her whole class rolling around on the floor. She tells them that their friend Alfred Alligator has injured his tail. He won't be able to return to school unless they can be trusted to be gentle with one another. Everyone misses Alfred very much, but will they be able to convince Miss Beanie that they can follow the Golden Rule?*

## Circle Time Session 2 Preparation

Re-read the book and focus on the thoughtful ways in which the animals look after Alfred.

## What you need

A speaking object

Alfred Alligator and other animal finger puppets

A selection of toy animals and dolls

Calming music

**Adult:** *Hello Alfred, do you have something that you want to say to the class?*

**Alfred:** *Yes, I have a new red bike and when I was riding down a hill something unexpected happened...*

**Adult:** *Oh Alfred, I think I might have heard the story about you and your new red bike.*
(Turn to the children.)
*Does anyone remember what happened to Alfred when he forgot to use his brakes?*

- Talk about the events in the book until the children are ready for an activity that focuses their attention on how we show that we are kind and gentle. Give out a number of fluffy toys so that they are spread out around the group. Ask the children to pass them gently to the person next to them and keep on passing them until you call out instructions. These could include: the toys are hungry, the toys have a bad tummy ache, the toys are tired, the toys have hurt their paws and so on. The children holding the toys must look after them in an appropriate manner.

### Warming up

- Using the speaking object, ask the children to complete the following sentence: 'When I don't feel very well, I like...'
(They might reply: a cuddle, hot chocolate, hot water bottle etc.)

### Opening up

- Teach the children the traditional lullaby:

  *Hush-a-bye baby on the treetop,*
  *When the wind blows, the cradle will rock,*
  *When the bough breaks, the cradle will fall,*
  *Down will come baby, cradle and all.*

- Put the children into pairs or small groups and distribute the toy animals and dolls. Tell the children that each of these toys has had a nasty time just like Alfred Alligator and needs to be looked after and put to bed. Sing the lullaby again. The children should hold the toys in an appropriate way. Ask them to think of a story to act out to the rest of the class that will show how they will take gentle care of their toy and make it feel better.

### Cheering up

- Congratulate the children on how gently they cared for their toys. Tell them that we all deserve to be treated with gentleness and consideration, which often means being patient and restrained in

the way we treat other people. Tell them about occasions when you have noticed how gently they behaved.

## Calming down

- Ask the children to sit comfortably with their eyes closed and their hands in their laps. Play some calming music and show them how to concentrate on their breathing and make it slow and steady.

# Extension activities

## Role-play area

- Make your role-play area into a doctor's surgery, a veterinary surgery, a hospital or a baby's nursery. Talk to the children about how each 'patient' got hurt and all the things they might like to do to make everyone feel better.

## Visitors

- Invite a parent with a baby to come into the classroom and talk to the children about caring for the baby and the importance of being gentle.

## Pet care

- Ask the children to choose their ideal pet and research how it should be cared for. This information can be made into little handmade books or a wall display.

## Shape books

- Cut out a book in the shape of Alfred Alligator and ask each child to contribute one page that shows a situation in which they would be gentle with him.

# We work hard...

## Circle time session 1

### Circle Time Session 1 Preparation

Read the book to the children so that they are familiar with the characters and the plot. Encourage your children to re-enact the story using the finger puppets.

### What you need

- A copy of the book *We Work Hard, We Don't Waste Time*
- A speaking object
- Animal finger puppets or masks

### Meeting up

- Ask the children to choose one job and to mime it. See if you can guess which job some of the children have chosen.

### Warming up

- Using the speaking object, ask the children to complete the following sentence, 'I worked hard when I...'

### Opening up

- Re-read the section of the story when Alfred realises there is no time to show his box of treasures. Begin to talk about how Alfred Alligator must have been feeling at home-time and then use the following script to include the story characters in your circle meeting.

**Adult:** *I've just had a thought! We don't need to guess how Alfred was feeling because he is right here and can tell us himself!*
(Put Alfred on your finger.)
*Hello, Alfred, you were very excited about the baby weren't you?*

**Alfred:** *I brought in a whole box of baby treasures but Louis Lion wasted time and spoiled my big surprise!*
(Make Alfred look very 'down' and dejected.)

- Continue in this way for a little while and then ask for volunteers to come forward and become the other story characters by wearing the appropriate finger puppets. Each character can tell Louis Lion how he can be difficult sometimes.

- Develop this activity by putting the children into small groups. Give each group the task of re-enacting the way in which Louis Lion spoils everybody's day by wasting time. (You can use puppets, masks or toys.) Watch some of the plays and ask the children if they have any suggestions that might help Louis Lion. They can act these out if there is time. Finally, thank the children for helping Louis Lion learn how to work better with the rest of the group.

# We don't waste time

## Cheering up

- Praise any children who have been working hard recently. Ask others to nominate classmates who they think should be commended.

## Calming down

- Use the following script to guide the children through a calming visualisation.

*'Sit with both feet on the floor. Make sure you are comfortable and relaxed.*

*Close your eyes and sit very still.*

*Listen to your breathing; can you feel the air going in and out? Just listen to your breath for a moment and let your mind be very still.*

*Take a long slow breath and let it out very gently, like this. Your breathing is slow and calm. Your mind is calm. Calm and slow. Calm and relaxed.'*
(Pause.)

*'Now it is time to begin to notice sounds around you.*

*Shake your shoulders and arms.*

*Wiggle your fingers and toes.*

*Wiggle your knees and elbows.*

*Open your eyes when you are ready and sit quietly for a moment.'*

# Circle time session 2

## Meeting up

- Smile at the child who is sitting next to you and ask them to smile at the child on their other side, and so on, until the smile is passed around the group and returned to you.

## Warming up

- Ask the children to think about all of the things that we need each day at school. Using the speaking object, ask the children to name one thing. For example, we need brushes for painting, and we need blocks for counting.

## The story

*On Monday Alfred Alligator is bursting with news – his mother has just had a baby. He brings in a special box of treasures to share with the class. But Louis Lion wastes so much time that there is no opportunity for sharing at the end of that day, or on Tuesday, or on Wednesday. When, finally, there is time on Thursday and Miss Beanie asks Alfred to share the box, he has taken it home again because he thought no-one was interested. Will the class get to see his treasures?*

## Circle Time Session 2 Preparation

- Re-read the book and discuss how the main characters must be feeling as the story goes along and at the end of the story. Go through what Miss Beanie says and ask the children if they can guess how she must have been feeling.

- Hide a number of small objects around the room and keep a note of where you have hidden them.

## What you need

A speaking object

A number of small classroom objects

A sand timer

Animal finger puppets and some sticker-badges hidden in a 'treasure' box

### Opening up

- Read the section from the story where everybody is held up because Louis Lion has hidden his clothes. Talk about Louis' behaviour and how Alfred must have been feeling.

- Talk about how long it takes to find things that have been lost. Tell the children that you have hidden some things around the classroom. Show them the sand timer and say that you are going to find out just how long it takes to find them all.

- Choose volunteers to find the hidden items and time how long it takes them. Ask the children if they have any stories to tell about things that have been lost at home. Talk about the ways in which their families keep important things safe and easy to locate.

### Cheering up

- Show the children the 'treasure' box containing sticker badges. Put Mona Monkey on your finger and use her to praise a hardworking child. You could use a script like this:

  **Adult:** *Who's this inside the box? Oh, it's Mona Monkey. Say hello to the children, Mona.*

  **Mona:** *Hello children. Hello, Jemma. I have noticed that you have been working very hard at the number table. I think that you should be given a badge for all that hard work.*
  (Turn Mona so that she is close to your ear.)

  *Please can I have a badge to give out?*

  **Adult:** *Of course you can, Mona. Come forward Jemma and let Mona give you a badge.*

- This can continue until all of the puppets have made a choice.

### Calming down

- Ask the children to think of the feeling they have after a busy day at school or after completing a difficult project. Help them to recall the satisfaction at a job well done and how they can relax, clear their minds and unwind. Ask them to picture a clear, green playing field on a summer day, to loosen their shoulders, breathe deeply, and enjoy the sense of peace.

# Extension activities

## Beat the clock!

- Put the children into small groups and use a sand timer to see how many repetitions of a task they can do in one minute. For instance, how many bricks can they build into a tower? How many times can they run around two cones? How many letters or numbers can they write? Ask the children to predict how many they think they will achieve. Discuss what they had to do to get as many as they could – concentrate, work hard and so on. How did it feel? How did they feel when they had completed a task? What happened if they lost concentration or messed about? Use this discussion to talk about the Golden Rule.

## Sorting game

- Put the children into groups to sort the picture cards on page 37. They show the animals working hard at some tasks and not so hard at others. The children can then discuss how they used evidence in the pictures to make their decisions.

## Targets

- Decide on one skill that you need to work on as a class. Use a class target chart to display a sticker every time the class works towards this target. Make the target simple and achievable. Everyone will have to concentrate and work hard but will feel proud when they succeed.

## Things we need

- Prepare two trays so that one is a selection of neatly-presented classroom equipment and the other is a messy combination of equipment and useless junk. Ask for two volunteers – one for each tray – and give them the same task to do. For example, 'Find me three things we need for maths' or 'Show me two things we use when we are doing art'. Which child is able to complete these tasks with ease and which one finds it difficult? Can anyone tell you why it is more difficult for one child? Point out that we can waste a lot of learning time when we hunt for things that haven't been put away properly. It is everyone's responsibility to look after classroom equipment.

# We are kind and helpful...

## Circle Time Session 1 Preparation

Read the book to the children so that they are familiar with the characters and the plot. Give the children time to discuss their opinions about Elsa's behaviour and her attitude to other people's distress. Highlight the conversation that takes place when Miss Beanie explains why she cannot trust Elsa.

## What you need

- A copy of the book *We Are Kind And Helpful, We Don't Hurt Anybody's Feelings*
- Elsa Elephant and other finger puppets
- A selection of balls
- A speaking object
- A big empty box or basket

## Circle time session 1

### Meeting up

- Choose one child to stand in the middle of the circle and give them a ball. Chant the words, 'Turn around, turn around, turn around and now sit down,' as you turn them around and then help them to sit cross-legged on the floor. They must now roll the ball to the child who is sitting straight ahead of them. Next, they must go and fetch the child who has received the ball and repeat the 'turn around' chant before sitting in the place of the child who now holds the ball. The child who is holding the ball then rolls it straight ahead and the game continues.

### Warming up

- Ask each child to remember an occasion when they have been helpful or kind. Using the speaking object, ask them to complete the following sentence: 'I was helpful when…' Allow shy children to 'pass'. Comment positively on the contributions that have been made by the class as a whole.

### Opening up

- Put Elsa Elephant on your finger and let her mess up your hair with her trunk while you say, 'Ouch' and 'Stop that, Elsa'. Let her whisper in your ear and then tell the children the shocking and unkind things that she has been saying. Your script could go like this:

**Adult:** *Elsa, that's a very unkind thing to say. You won't believe this, children, but Elsa says that my cardigan makes me look like a big fluffy bear instead of a teacher. What do you think of that?*
(Wiggle Elsa up and down.)
*Look at her now, shaking with laughter because she thinks it's really funny to be rude to a teacher. What do you think we should do with Elsa? Who would like to come up and be one of the other animals and try to help Elsa to be kind and thoughtful?*

- Give each volunteer a puppet while you keep Elsa on your finger and speak for her.

# We don't hurt anybodys feelings

## The story

*There's a big surprise in store for the whole class except for Elsa Elephant who has behaved badly and not thought of the feelings of others. Miss Beanie gives the surprise to Gino Giraffe and Zelda Zebra to look after – not Elsa. A chance encounter finally allows Elsa to prove to Miss Beanie that she too can be kind and helpful. She learns just how nice it can be to be trusted to follow the Golden Rule.*

### Cheering up

- Think of some recent occasions when the class has had to co-operate and praise the way in which they have helped one another. These may include tidying up after art, putting away books, finding a lost coat, watering plants etc.

### Calming down

- Ask the children to hold hands in the group. Gently squeeze the hand of the child next to you and ask them to pass the gentle squeeze on round the group. Repeat this with a smile. Unclasp hands and thank the children for being kind and helpful to one another.

## Circle time session 2

### Meeting up

- Go round the group and point to each child in turn and tell them that they have to pretend to be holding a rabbit, a heavy stone or a big, wobbly jelly. Call out each item in turn. When they are called, the children with that item must swap places and move as if they are carrying their rabbit, stone or jelly.

### Circle Time Session 2 Preparation

Re-read the book, taking extra care to emphasise an appropriate tone of voice for all the speaking parts. Use the finger puppets to re-enact scenes from the story.

### Warming up

- Ask the children to think of an occasion when someone has helped or been kind to them. Give them some ideas – Daddy made toast, my sister zipped up my coat, Mummy carried my lunch box. Pass the speaking object round the group so that everybody has the opportunity to contribute their example of kindness.

### Opening up

- Talk about some of the times when we need a little bit of help – finding something that is lost, learning something new, tidying up etc.

- Put Gino Giraffe on your finger and let him talk to the children.

## What you need

Elsa Elephant and other finger puppets

A speaking object

A selection of classroom soft toys or dolls

Some golden star badges or certificates

Some peaceful music (Most music stores stock compilations of relaxing music.)

**Gino:** *Hello, I'm Gino and one bit of me is very unusual. Who knows what is special about giraffes?*

(Take suggestions from the children.)

*Yes, that's right, I have a very long neck and that means that I need a very long scarf to keep my neck warm. And that, children, is what my problem is all about. I have lost my scarf and I don't even know where to start searching.*

**Adult:** *Who would like to make a little play to show how you might help Gino to find his scarf?*

- Give Gino to a group of children who might be able to help him. Take another puppet and give it a problem that could be solved with a little help. Repeat this with the other finger puppets until each one is part of a group of children who will show how helpful they can be. Ask them to make up a very short play about being kind and helpful as they look after each puppet's needs. Give them a few minutes to work on their play.

- Now ask for volunteers to show their play to the rest of the class. As they do so, note down some of the words they use to give and receive help. Thank the children for their plays and repeat some of the things that you have heard them say. For example, 'Let's try it this way,' 'Would it help if…' or 'Shall we do it together?'

- Use the phrases again but now use a cross, negative tone of voice. Talk with the children about which words and tones of voice help them to feel good about being helped and which make them uncomfortable. Read what Elsa says on page 11 when she looks at Gino and Zelda's tower: 'That tower is too tall and it's all the wrong shape'. Say it in different ways. Is there a kind tone of voice that would make it sound better? What would the rabbit do if Elsa spoke the words on page 25, 'Come here little rabbit', in a loud, cross voice?

- Give the children a problem that you need help with. It might be an untidy book corner, people interrupting each other when you try to talk at carpet time or classroom resources in the wrong places. Ask for suggestions. They can answer with, 'Would it help if….' Ask all of the children to use the special, kindly tone of voice.

### Cheering up

- Thank the children for being so very kind and helpful. Ask if any children would like to nominate a friend or classmate for a special golden badge because they are often kind and helpful. Ask for the story of each act of kindness and celebrate it as a group.

- Remind the children that you have been thinking about the difference that someone's tone of voice can make to how we feel. Say that you are going to play some happy, peaceful music because that has a similar effect. Play the music until you see that the children are quietly relaxed and then take them calmly to the next activity in the day.

# Extension activities

### Before and after

- Photocopy two copies of the elephant mask (see page 34). Ask the children to contribute words that describe Elsa's personality at the beginning of the book and list these on the first mask. You can add some of the things that she says such as, 'I don't care'. Use the second mask to list the opposite words to show how differently we view her when she has learned to be kind and helpful.

### People who help us

- Ask the children to draw a picture of one of the people who work in your school. Cut these out, mount them on card and write each person's name underneath. Compile a list of all the kind and helpful things that each person has done for the children in your class. Make them into a book or classroom display.

### How can I help?

- Fold pieces of paper into four so that they can be made into short cartoon strips. Ask each child to use the first section to draw a picture of a problem – a wilted flower, a sick animal, an untidy bookshelf etc. In the second section, they can draw a person with a thought bubble to show that they have noticed the problem. In the third, ask them to draw the person being kind and helpful and use a speech bubble to show what they say. Lastly, they can draw a picture of the problem solved.

### Soft or scratchy

- Cut out letter shapes using materials with soft or rough textures (fabric and sandpaper) so that you can make the words kind or unkind. Use these words as headings for a list of *kind* and *unkind* words that the children can collect.

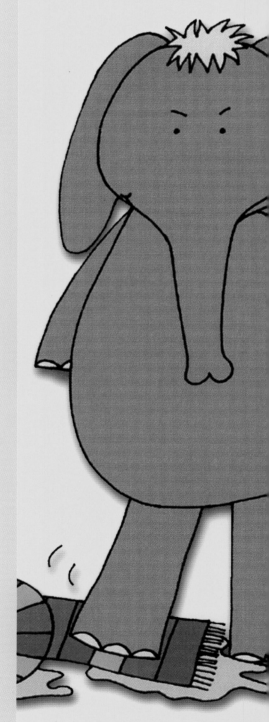

# We listen...

## Circle time session 1

use the five steps of circle time to focus on learning about listening skills

### Circle Time Session 1 Preparation

Read the book to your class so that the children are familiar with the plot and the characters. When reading it for the first time, stop at the end of page 10 and ask them to guess what Gino is trying to tell Zelda. Encourage them to predict different endings for the story.

### What you need

- A copy of the book *We Listen, We Don't Interrupt*
- Make two photocopies of the animal cards from page 35-36 and cut them out
- Zelda Zebra and other finger puppets
- A speaking object – a decorated egg, a small cuddly toy or a shell
- A one-minute sand timer
- Badges, made using the 'I'm a good listener' template on page 34
- Calming music

### Meeting up

- Give each child an animal card. (Make sure that there are two of each animal so that all the children will be able to find a partner.) Ask them to look carefully at their card and remember which animal they have. Tell them to stand up and put the card on their chair. Now ask the children to mingle in the middle of the circle and make the animal noise that is appropriate for their card. (They don't need to be noisy!) They need to move around making the noise until they have found their partner. Once they have found their partner, they must sit down together.

- For the next part of the game, they will find a different card on their seat and will be ready to play again. Play the game a few times and then talk about what made it easy or difficult to find their partner. They may suggest things like: getting too close before making their noise, taking turns to make their noise, being too loud, stopping and listening to another person, looking at the person they are listening to.

### Warming up

- Pass the speaking object around the circle and give each child the opportunity to complete this sentence: 'I like to listen to…'

- You can ask them to add their reason for liking the sound they have chosen. For example, 'I like listening to the sea because it reminds me of my holidays.' You could try this with 'I don't like listening to…'

### Opening up

- Put Zelda Zebra on your finger and use her to model different kinds of listening behaviour by demonstrating how she can lean forward, nod and make 'I am listening' noises to show that she is being attentive to what is being said. Show how she can wriggle, look the other way, wander off and be generally inattentive!

# We don't interrupt

- Show the children the sand timer and tell them that they have one minute to chat and find something out about each other. You can give them a subject: hobbies, holidays, what happened at their birthday party etc.

- Ask for volunteers to come forward and show their interview to the rest of the group. Make sure that the children can see that Zelda is listening attentively. Thank your volunteers for being brave and entertaining.

## Cheering up

- Praise the children for listening attentively to one another and for remembering the things that they have told one another. Be specific and give them examples of particularly good listening. Tell the children that you will be looking out for examples of these behaviours in the next few days because the feeling of being listened to is a very happy feeling. Show the children the 'good listener' badges and promise that you will be giving them out during the next few days.

## Calming down

- Ask the children to close their eyes, hands on knees, with palms facing upwards and their fingers slightly curled. (This relaxes the shoulders and most children find it easier to sit still in this position.) Begin playing relaxing music and ask the children to listen and picture playing in the sunshine somewhere nice. After a couple of minutes, you can calmly bring them back to the room and thank them for a lovely circle meeting.

# Circle time session 2

## Meeting up

- Hold up the illustration on page 29 of the story and talk about the party things on the table. Look at the slice of delicious chocolate cake and ask if anyone knows how it is made and what it is made from. Tell the children that they are all going to be an ingredient of chocolate cake and then go round the group and tell each child which ingredient they will be: butter, eggs, flour, sugar or cocoa.

Circle Time Session 2
Preparation
Re-read the book and talk about the personality of each character. Can the children think of words to describe Gino and Zelda to show how different they are? Which one do the children like best? Who would they choose as a friend?

## What you need

A speaking object

Zelda Zebra, Gino Giraffe, and other animal finger puppets

A tape/cd of orchestral music

(Chopin and Bach are recommended.)

- When you say the word 'eggs', the children who are eggs must change places with someone who is also an egg. Then, all the 'flour' children must changes places and so on until the whole group is sitting in another place.

### Warming up

- Using the speaking object, ask the children to complete the following sentence: 'I like parties because…'

### Opening up

- Ask two children to come forward to be Gino and Zelda. Give them the appropriate finger puppets. Ask the other children to give you some words to describe these two characters. Point out that some words tell us how they look, and others show how they behave. Continue the conversation like this:

   **Adult:** *Who can think of a word that would tell us what Zelda looks like?*
   **Child:** *I think she looks stripy.*
   **Zelda:** *Yes, I am stripy and I think that stripes are very pretty indeed.*

- Steer the conversation so that you are talking about Zelda's behaviour and ask the children if they have any advice that might help Zelda to become a better listener. Give the children some everyday scenarios in which they can model good listening. Skills might include showing interest through attentive body language, repeating comments back to the speaker, questioning and not changing the subject. They can use masks when they act out these scenarios.

- Do the same for Gino and ask if the children have any advice that will make him more assertive. Can the children give you some words that describe how it feels to be ignored and interrupted?

   **Adult:** *Now that we have helped Gino and Zelda, can we add some more words that describe the way it feels when we have been listened to? These are much happier words.*

### Cheering up

- Thank the children for their useful advice and tell them that you are very impressed with the way in which they are gaining such excellent listening skills. Praise individual children for their good contributions but ensure that the whole group feels proud to be such good listeners.

- Encourage the children to practise their skills at home and let you know if they have found that good listening works at home as well as at school.

## Calming down

- Tell the children that you are going to end the circle meeting with some music. Ask them to sit quietly and to shut their eyes while they listen. Tell them that there will be no words to distract them and that all they need to do is listen attentively and let the music wrap them up in its special mood and beauty. When the music is finished, ask them to give their toes and hands a little shake. Then they can roll their shoulders and head, take three long, deep breaths and quietly go on to their next lesson.

# Extension activities

## Puppet plays

- Give each group a selection of finger puppets or masks. Ask them to re-tell part of the story using their own words. Talk about the important message in the story and then ask them to make up their own plays about listening and show these to the rest of the class.

## Story writing

- As a whole class, in groups or individually, invite the children to write a different ending for the story or create their own tale about listening using these characters in a different setting. Make them into books to be shared in the classroom.

## Animal characters

- In groups or individually, encourage the children to draw, paint or collage one of the animals and write words to describe them beneath the picture.

## Rattle and scrunch

- Make a collection of items that make a noise when you do something to them – crisp packet, bells, keys, paper etc. Put them in a box so that they are hidden from the children. Put your hand into the box and make each sound. Ask the children to guess what's inside. Talk about what they had to do in order to guess: sit very still, be quiet, concentrate, think etc.

# We look after property...

## Circle time session 1

### Circle Time Session 1 Preparation

Read the book to the class so that they are familiar with the story and characters. You could stop reading at the end of page 10 and ask the children if they can guess what Miss Beanie's good idea might be.

### What you need

- A copy of the book *We Look After Property, We Don't Damage Things*
- A speaking object
- Animal finger puppets
- Badges, made using the 'I look after things' template on page 34
- A selection of animal toys, puppets or masks
- Some calming music (You will find a range of relaxation compilations in most music stores.)

### Meeting up

- Read pages 4, 5, 6 and 7 and show the pictures to the children. Go round the group and tell each child that they will be a different colour of super, glittery play-dough – red, yellow or blue. When you call out 'blue', all the children who are that colour must change places with one another. Repeat this with yellow and red. When you call out 'Tidy-up time, everyone' the whole group must go into a huddle in the middle of the circle until you call 'now', when they must quickly find a new seat.

### Warming up

- Talk to the children about all the different activities that happen in Miss Beanie's classroom. Using the speaking object, ask the children to complete the following sentence: 'My favourite time at school is…' (Cutting out, painting, playing with play-dough etc).

### Opening up

- Put the children into small groups and help them to make up some little plays based on different scenes from the story. Ask for volunteers to show their plays to the rest of the class.

- Give out the finger puppets so that the animals can watch the plays too. Ask the children to help the puppets by telling them how we all look after things in the classroom. (There are places for everything to go, boxes to keep small things together, different areas for different activities. This helps with tidying up at the end of a session.)

- Talk about what the classroom would be like if we didn't do these things. Ask for suggestions for how we could look after things in the classroom and make it a nicer place to be. Make plans to carry out some of these ideas.

### Cheering up

- Make sure your badges are ready (from page 34). Put on a pair of finger puppets and use them to give out badges to the children who always take care of classroom property. Your script might read like this:

# We don't damage things

**Alfred:** *Come here, Elsa, and let's think about who should be given a badge.* (Put your hands together so that Alfred and Elsa appear to be having a conversation.)

**Elsa:** *Alfred and I have had a chat and we have decided that Shaheen has earned this badge. Let's give her a clap!*

- Continue with the remaining puppets.

## Calming down

- Ask the children to lie on the floor in an uncomfortable and untidy way but without touching anyone else. Play some calming music and ask them to stretch out and 'tidy' themselves up until they are rested and comfortable. Allow them to lie in this relaxed position for a few minutes as they listen to the music. Then you can ask them to stand up slowly and quietly and go on to the next activity.

## Circle time session 2

### Meeting up

- Tell the children that you are in Miss Beanie's classroom. You are going to mime some of the activities that take place there while the children copy your actions. Talk them through the mimes by saying, *'Gino is cutting up the play-dough'* and *'Alfred is playing with the car jigsaw puzzle'*. When you say, *'Miss Beanie says, "Tidy-up time, children",'* everyone must stand up and quickly sit in a different place.

### Warming up

- Using the speaking object, ask the children to complete the sentence: *'My most precious thing is my…'* (They might say: my new toy car, rabbit, silver necklace etc.)

### Opening up

- Show the children your box of precious things and tell them why each thing is important to you. Ask them to tell you about their precious things (or tell each other in pairs).

## The story

*The animals in Miss Beanie's class are all having a great time with play-dough, puzzles and paper play. But when it comes to tidying away, they're not so careful and things end up in the bin or are all muddled up. At the end of the week, when Miss Beanie says they can go and play, there's nothing left. She has thought of a clever way to help them appreciate an important Golden Rule.*

## Circle Time Session 2 Preparation

Re-read the book with the class and focus on how Miss Beanie must have been feeling as the story goes along. What was she feeling when she saw the way in which the materials had been treated? Why did she frown?

## What you need

A speaking object

A box containing some things that are precious to you: a photo of your family, an ornament, your favourite book, a piece of jewellery etc

27

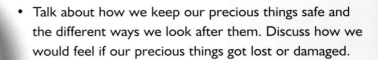

- Talk about how we keep our precious things safe and the different ways we look after them. Discuss how we would feel if our precious things got lost or damaged.

- Find some things from your classroom that haven't been looked after properly. Pass them round the circle for the children to look at. Talk about what happened to them, why and how they could have been looked after more carefully. Ask the children to suggest how everyone can stop this from happening to other things in the classroom. Make some plans together and discuss who will check that things are being looked after well. Would some children like to be monitors or classroom helpers? Do they think a rota would be a good idea? Would they like you to make some certificates or badges to show who has looked after property particularly well?

## Cheering up

- Thank the children for their suggestions and pass the finger puppets around the group so that everyone has the opportunity to use one to tell the class which part of the circle meeting they most enjoyed.

## Calming down

- Stand up and hold hands in the circle. Swing your arms as you chant, 'We are lovely and very, very special'. On the word 'special', everyone must lift their arms as high as they can. Lower your arms and repeat the sentence.

# Extension activities

## Story-telling

- Ask the children to tell the rest of the group about times when they, or members of their family, have lost something important. What happened because it was lost? Did Dad ever lose his car keys? Did Mum ever lose her glasses? How did they go about sorting out the problem? How long did it take to find the lost items? Were they ever found or did they need to be replaced? Prompt the children by telling a story of your own if necessary. Ask the children to make up a short story about something that was lost and found. This can be a cartoon story, writing with a single illustration or a play acted out in a drama lesson.

- Ask the children to bring in a precious object to show to the rest of the class. Encourage them to talk about how they take care of it and keep it safe. Be sure that these objects are kept in a safe place while they are in your classroom.

- Put some bits of classroom equipment into a box or tub and cover them up with torn-up newspaper or tissue paper. Allow one child at a time to dig into the tub and pull out an object. They can talk about how we care for it and show the rest of the class where it is kept and how it is stored to keep it as good as new.

- Make little books that tell a 'days of the week' story about how a toy loses its parts through neglect and accidents. Children could do this as a group and take a day each. An example might be:

*On Monday, Freddy the fire engine had smart red paint and four black wheels but Tamsin trod on him and one of his wheels fell off. On Tuesday, Freddy the fire engine had smart red paint and three black wheels.*

A picture on each page would show how Freddy becomes more and more unusable until he is saved by Mr Tibbs, the caretaker.

# We are honest...

## Circle time session 1

### Meeting up

- Ask the children to stand up. Tell them that you are going to give them some instructions and you are going to show them what you want them to do at the same time. Give them some simple instructions: put your hands in the air, stand on one foot, wiggle your fingers etc. Before you give the instructions, say the words, 'Mona says…'

### Warming up

- Put on the finger puppets and show the children how they dance with excitement at the very mention of a school concert. Ask the children to share what they like about school by completing the following sentence: 'The part of school that I like best is…' Use the speaking object and allow the children to 'pass' if they feel too shy to speak.

### Opening up

- Put on the finger puppets and use the following script to lead the children through this part of the circle meeting:

**Mona:** *When we tell the truth, we are telling what really happened.*
**Alfred:** *We call this being honest.*
**Zelda:** *Let's think about what that means.*
**Adult:** *I am going to do something and then I will be honest and tell you what I really did.*

Pick up a classroom toy such as a red toy car. Pick it up and put it down again. Tell the children, 'I picked up the red car and I put it down again'. Ask some children to choose a toy, do something with it and then tell the class what they have done. Thank them for being truthful and honest. Now ask the children if they thought this was a very easy, simple activity.

**Adult:** *Yes, it was easy for all of you to do, wasn't it? But things can get very complicated when we don't tell the truth. Next time we'll play this game again but we'll do it differently.*

## Circle Time Session 1 Preparation

Read the book to your class so that the children are familiar with the plot and the characters. Encourage them to predict different endings for the story. If your class is familiar with the Golden Rules, tell them that the book is about one of the rules and ask them if they know which one it is.

## What you need

- A copy of the book *We Are Honest, We Don't Cover Up The Truth*
- A speaking object: a decorated egg, a small cuddly toy or a shell
- Mona Monkey and other finger puppets
- A selection of classroom toys

# We don't cover up the truth

## Cheering up

- Thank the children for their contributions to the circle meeting. Tell them that you are being very honest when you tell them how wonderful they all are. Pass a smile around the group by smiling at the child next to you and asking them to pass it on until everyone has given and received one.

## Calming down

- Use this script for a relaxation exercise:

*'Sit with both feet on the floor. Make sure you are comfortable and warm and will not be disturbed.*
*Close your eyes and sit very still.*
*Listen to your breathing. Can you feel the air going in and out of your nose? Just listen to your breath for a moment and let your mind become very still.*
*Take a long slow breath and let it out gently, like this. Your breathing is slow and calm. Your mind is calm. Calm and slow, calm and relaxed.'*
(Continue with the slow breathing for about one minute and then quietly bring the children back.)
*'Shake your shoulders and arms.*
*Wiggle your fingers and toes.*
*Wiggle your knees and your elbows.*
*Open your eyes when you are ready and sit quietly for a moment.'*

# Circle time session 2

## Meeting up

- Tell the children that you are going to play 'Mona says' again but, this time, you are going to make the game a little harder. Mona usually tells the truth, but sometimes she says things that are not true. Tell the children that when Mona is untruthful they must copy what you do and not what you say. They have to watch you very carefully.

- Play the game as you did in the last session but, now and then, give a verbal instruction while doing something different. For example, you might say, 'Clap your hands' while flapping them around your head. Any child who 'believes' what you say and follows the verbal instruction has to sit down until they are allowed back into the game.

## The story

*Miss Beanie and her class are getting ready for Thursday's concert. With props and costumes to make, everyone is excited. But Mona Monkey is enjoying playing so much that she does not want to follow instructions. Miss Beanie has to find a way to help Mona learn another important Golden Rule so that she can join in the fun of the concert with everyone else.*

## Circle Time Session 2 Preparation

Re-read the story to your class with a focus on the dishonest things that Mona says and does. Discuss how Miss Beanie trusts and believes her until Mona is faced with the consequences of her behaviour.

## What you need

Mona Monkey and other finger puppets

A speaking object

31

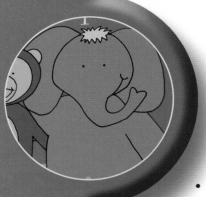

## Warming up

- Remind the children that the story is about getting ready for a school concert. Tell them that concerts are great fun. There is singing and dancing and acting. Ask for a show of hands to find out how many children have watched a concert.

- Ask the children to share what they would like to do if you had a school concert. Ask them to complete the sentence, 'If I were in a school concert, I would like to…' Use the speaking object and allow children to 'pass' if they feel too shy to speak.

## Opening up

- Put on a finger puppet and 'help' them to pick up a classroom toy. Do something with it, then tell the children that you have done something completely different. For example, 'help' Mona to pick up a toy train and make *choo-choo* train noises as you do so. Now continue:

    **Adult:** *Mona picked up a toy lorry and I made brrrm, brrrm noises.*

- Do this again with some other toys. Ask some children to choose a toy and copy what you have done. Ask the children in the circle to describe what has been going on. They will get a little confused in their account of events, so allow them to.

    **Adult:** *Was this activity as easy as the one in our previous circle time session? Who got a little bit confused? Yes, so did I! That's because telling lies is very confusing for other people.*

- Remind the children of the main events in the story of Mona Monkey. Can they remember any of the lies that she told Miss Beanie? Was Miss Beanie a kind teacher or a mean one?

- Talk about the way in which Miss Beanie trusted Mona to be honest. Show the children that trust means that we are kind and think the best of other people. This means that our feelings are hurt when we discover that our trust has been misplaced. What do the children think Miss Beanie was feeling when she realised just how many times Mona had lied to her?

- If you feel that the class is ready, you can now talk about their feelings in situations when truth/untruth was an issue.

## Cheering up

- Re-read page 30 of the story. Tell the children that they can give themselves a clap and that you know of a few reasons why. List some of the things that they have done well recently and focus on any examples of honesty.

## Calming down

- Give out the finger puppets so that they are spread around the group. Play a cheerful tune. While it is playing, the children with the finger puppets must make them dance along. The last puppet still dancing when the music stops must be given to the next child on the right without a puppet. Continue for a few rounds until everyone is in a happy frame of mind. Close the game by asking everyone to stand up and stretch up high, as if they are smiling and waving at the sun, before relaxing and standing floppy and relaxed, ready for the next part of the day.

# Extension activities

## True or false

- Give each child two pictures of an animal, chosen from the animal cards on pages 35 and 36, mounted on card. Ask them to colour in the animals. On one of the pictures, let the children write (or you can scribe) a sentence describing a fact about the picture that is true, eg 'The hippo is orange'. On the other, do the same with a fact that is not true, eg 'The hippo is purple'. Now they must swap their pictures with a friend who has to label each one 'true' or 'untrue'.

## The bigger picture

- Show the children a poster, artwork or book illustration. Display a series of statements about the picture. The children must tell you if the statements are true, false/untrue or impossible to answer/not enough evidence. For example: Mona is a monkey (*true*). Miss Beanie is a horse (*false*). Mona had porridge for breakfast (*don't know/not enough evidence*).

## Don't cover up

- Ask the children to cover their eyes while you hide some animal finger puppets or small toys. Put them in clear view. Choose a child and count how many seconds it takes him to find the puppets. Repeat the exercise, but this time cover the puppets up and hide them so that they will be more difficult to find. Show the children how many more seconds it has taken to find the hidden puppets. Point out that dishonesty makes the truth harder to find in just the same way.

## Miss Beanie in the hot seat

- Tell the children that you are going to pretend to be Miss Beanie and that they can ask you questions and find out a bit more about you. Then, ask for volunteers to come and sit in the hot seat. Let the volunteer choose one of the finger puppets. The group can ask the finger puppet some questions with the child there to 'help' it give answers.

# Elsa Elephant/Badges

Use with the Before and After activity on page 21 and the reward activities on page 23 and 26

# Animal Cards 1

Use with the Animal Cards activity on page 22 and 33

# Animal Cards 2

Use with the Animal Cards activity on page 22 and 33

# Sorting Game

Cut out the cards and use with the Sorting Game activity on page 17

# The Golden Rules Song

Words & Music by Sean Duggan

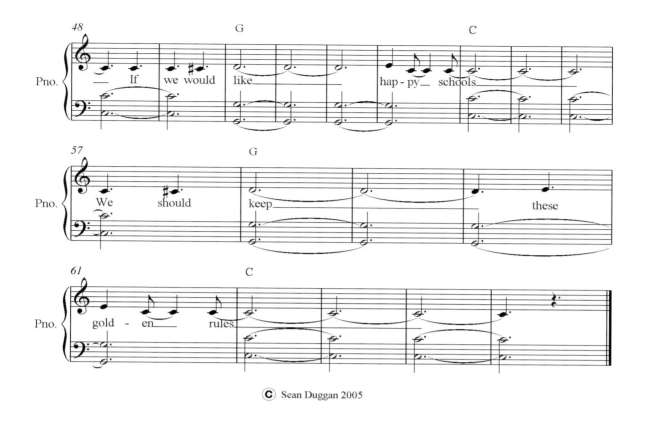

We are kind and helpful in what we do and say
If we act like this we'll make someone's day
We've got to think about what's on peoples' minds
And how we make them feel when we're helpful and kind

*Chorus:*
It's a Golden Rule that will help us all
Young or old, short or tall
If we would like happy schools
We must keep the Golden Rules

We like to tell the truth, about all we do
If we tell a lie, who's kidding who?
There's no-one else can see inside
So tell the truth, don't keep the facts inside
*Repeat Chorus*

We've got to try to listen, that's what our ears are for
And look at the person who's talking, we'll hear
even more
We've got to speak only when it's our turn
And be surprised – how much we learn
*Repeat Chorus*

We are gentle, and we don't hurt others
One big family, sisters and brothers
We should all feel safe, no need to fight
In a peaceful world, the future's bright
*Repeat Chorus*

We work hard, we don't waste our time
If we try our best, we end up doing fine
We will fulfil our every need
If we don't waste time, we're bound to succeed
*Repeat Chorus*

We don't damage things, that's because we care
We know some people do, they think it's a dare
They might think they're cool, when they're
acting the fool
They're spoiling our lives, and they're spoiling our school
*Repeat Chorus*

These charming Golden Rules books support parents, carers and teachers who wish to help their children love the Golden Rules

# The books in the series...

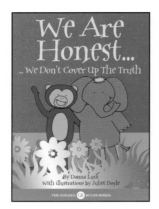
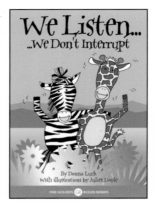
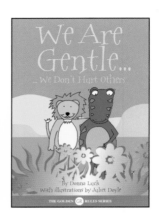

We Are Gentle ... We Don't Hurt Others

We Are Honest ... We Don't Cover Up The Truth

We Listen ... We Don't Interrupt

We are Kind and Helpful ... We Don't Hurt Anybody's Feelings

We Look After Property ... We Don't Damage Things

We Work Hard ... We Don't Waste Time

For more information about the Golden Rules and
helping children to care about them, contact:

Jenny Mosley Consultancies/Positive Press Ltd.
28A Gloucester Road, Trowbridge
Wiltshire BA14 0AA

Telephone: 01225 719204   Fax: 01225 712187
E-mail: positivepress@jennymosley.co.uk
Website: www.circle-time.co.uk